Pebble® Plus

Mighty Machines

Aircraft Carriers

by Matt Doeden

Consulting Editor: Gail Saunders-Smith, PhD

Capstone press®

Mankato, Minnesota

Pebble Plus is published by Capstone Press,
1710 Roe Crest Drive, North Mankato, Minnesota 56003
www.capstonepub.com

 Books published by Capstone Press are manufactured with paper
containing at least 10 percent post-consumer waste.

Library of Congress Cataloging-in-Publication Data
Doeden, Matt.
    Aircraft carriers / by Matt Doeden.
    p. cm.—(Pebble plus: mighty machines)
    Includes bibliographical references and index.
    ISBN-13: 978-0-7368-3656-2 (hardcover)
    ISBN-10: 0-7368-3656-X (hardcover)
    ISBN-13: 978-0-7368-5136-7 (softcover pbk.)
    ISBN-10: 0-7368-5136-4 (softcover pbk.)
    1. Aircraft carriers—United States—Juvenile literature. I. Title. II. Series.
V874.3.A37 2005
623.825'5'0973—dc22   2004012654

Summary: Simple text and photographs present aircraft carriers, their parts, and their crew.

Editorial Credits
Martha E. H. Rustad, editor; Molly Nei, set designer; Kate Opseth and Ted Williams, book designers;
    Jo Miller, photo researcher; Scott Thoms, photo editor

Photo Credits
Corbis/The Military Picture Library/Clive Newton, 6–7; Peter Turnley, 8–9
DVIC/PH1 David Dentry, 1; PH2 Steve Enfield, 14–15; PH2(AW) Tim W. Tow, 16–17; PH3 Narina Larry, 18–19
Getty Images Inc./Phil Mislinski, 10–11; U.S. Navy, cover, 4–5
Navy Photo by PH2 Christopher Vickers, 20–21
Ted Carlson/Fotodynamics, 12–13

Note to Parents and Teachers

The Mighty Machines set supports national standards related to science, technology,
and society. This book describes and illustrates aircraft carriers. The images support
early readers in understanding the text. The repetition of words and phrases helps early
readers learn new words. This book also introduces early readers to subject-specific
vocabulary words, which are defined in the Glossary section. Early readers may need
assistance to read some words and to use the Table of Contents, Glossary, Read More,
Internet Sites, and Index sections of the book.

Printed in the United States of America in North Mankato, Minnesota.
062013
007364R

Table of Contents

What Are Aircraft Carriers?

Aircraft carriers are
the largest ships in the navy.
Some are longer than
three football fields.

Aircraft carriers are
like floating airports.
Some carry as many
as 100 aircraft.

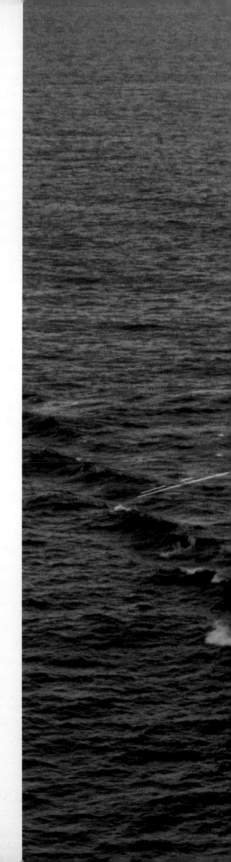

Aircraft take off
from aircraft carriers.
They also land
on aircraft carriers.

Parts of Aircraft Carriers

The main body
of an aircraft carrier
is called the hull.

hull

The flight deck is long
and flat. It looks like
an airport runway.

flight deck

island

The Crew

Thousands of people live and work on an aircraft carrier. They are called the crew.

Some crew members
fix aircraft.
Other crew members
fly aircraft.

Mighty Machines

Tugboats help aircraft
carriers come into port.
Aircraft carriers
are mighty machines.

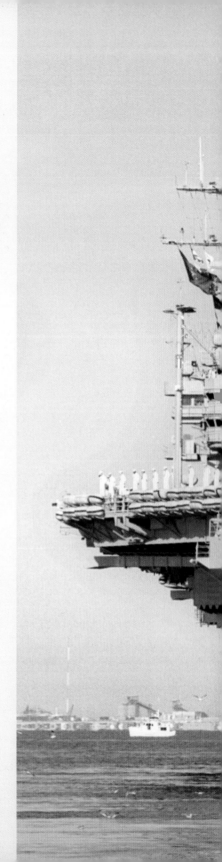

Glossary

aircraft—a vehicle that can fly; airplanes and helicopters take off from aircraft carriers.

crew—a team of people who work together

flight deck—the long, flat area on top of an aircraft carrier where planes can take off and land

hull—the main body of a ship; the hull is made of layers of steel.

island—a tower on an aircraft carrier that rises above the flight deck

navy—the military sea force of a country, including ships, aircraft, weapons, land bases, and people

pilot—a person who flies aircraft

port—a harbor where ships dock safely

tugboat—a small, powerful boat that pulls or pushes large ships

Read More

Amato, William. *Aircraft Carriers.* High-Tech Vehicles. New York: PowerKids Press, 2002.

Armentrout, David, and Patricia Armentrout. *Ships.* Transportation. Vero Beach, Fla.: Rourke, 2004.

Doeden, Matt. *The U.S. Navy.* The U.S. Armed Forces. Mankato, Minn.: Blazers, 2005.

Internet Sites

FactHound offers a safe, fun way to find Internet sites related to this book. All of the sites on FactHound have been researched by our staff.

Here's how:

1. Visit *www.facthound.com*

2. Type in this special code **073683656X** for age-appropriate sites. Or enter a search word related to this book for a more general search.

3. Click on the **Fetch It** button.

FactHound will fetch the best sites for you!

Index

Word Count: 124
Grade: 1
Early-Intervention Level: 15

The tower on an aircraft carrier is called the island. People in the island tell pilots when to take off and land.

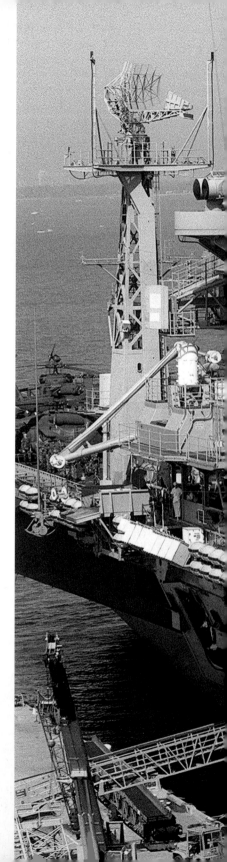